Blindsided by His Betrayal:

Surviving the Shock of Your Husband's Infidelity

By Caroline Madden, PhD

D1531485

TRAIN OF THOUGHT
PRESS

Publisher's Note

ISBN: 978-0-9861485-2-1
Library of Congress Number: 2016906383
TOTP: 12132019BBHB

Summary: Marriage therapist's advice on how to survive the shock of a husband's infidelity

TRAIN OF THOUGHT
PRESS

Other Books By Caroline Madden, PhD

Fool Me Once: Should I Take Back My Cheating Husband?

After a Good Man Cheats: How to Rebuild Trust & Intimacy With Your Wife

How to Go From Soul Mates to Roommates in 10 Easy Steps

Table of Contents

Introduction

Your husband cheated on you, and now you don't recognize yourself.

You used to be so together, so trusting. Now you're falling apart and doing things you would have never even considered doing, such as:

- Obsessively checking your husband's email and Facebook accounts
- Going through his cell phone history while he is in the shower
- Freaking out if he is 10 minutes late (or if you text him and he doesn't reply right away)
- Questioning whether you are attractive
- After a rare happy moment with your husband, getting really, *really* angry and raging at him out of nowhere

You're scared. Angry. Obsessive. Devastated.

One minute, you hope your marriage will make it. The next minute, you want to kill him. (And the other woman, too.)

All of this makes you feel like you are losing it. Sometimes you worry that you are going crazy. You wonder if you'll ever be the same again.

I am here to tell you that you are not crazy. You are having a normal reaction to an incredibly traumatizing experience. You might not have considered your husband's infidelity to be a traumatic event, but that's exactly what it is, and your reaction is a completely rational and expected response to such a painful experience.

I'm here to help you figure out what to do as you deal with these explosive emotions. It's important that you understand that your feelings—erratic and unpredictable as they may be—are normal. You need to understand why you feel the things you feel and what to do with those feelings.

I'll help you do exactly that. My name is Dr. Caroline Madden, and I'm an affair recovery specialist. I've worked as a licensed marriage and family therapist in Los Angeles for almost two decades, and in that time I have helped countless couples restore their marriages after infidelity.

I've also helped wives decide when it's time to throw in the towel. While I am a pro-marriage therapist (meaning I work primarily with couples who want to make the relationship work), I recognize that not all marriages can be or even should be saved.

As a wife myself, I would never tell another woman she should stay with a cheating husband just to keep the family intact. This is a book written by a woman, for women. To this end, I have made every effort to keep your needs in clear view.

This book does not take a position on whether or not you should stay in your marriage. (That is covered in my book: *Fool Me Once: Should I Take Back My Cheating Husband?*) The suggestions provided in *Blindsided by His Betrayal* will help you get through this difficult time, even if you decide to leave the marriage. It is geared towards helping you deal with your tumultuous emotions and make sound decisions.

Let's get started. WHY does his affair drive you so crazy? You feel this way for some very good reasons...

Chapter One:
How His Affair Has Changed You

You've just discovered your husband has been cheating on you.

I won't mince words; this is probably the worst time of your life. You may feel like a nuclear bomb has decimated your world and you are freefalling, grasping for something solid and trustworthy to hang onto.

There are a variety of reasons why husbands cheat and a myriad of affair types. However, as an affair recovery specialist I can tell you one factor remains constant: all wives in your situation lose a sense of self that is absolutely life-altering.

Not sure what I mean?

Pull up a photo of you and your husband (make sure it's from the timeframe during which you know he was cheating). Now look at it and take note of the feelings and thoughts that cross your mind.

There you are, the two of you smiling broadly. As you look at this photo, you will inevitably think:

I thought we were happy, but he was cheating on me.

How much of our relationship is a lie?

How did I miss this?

Can I trust my instincts?

If I didn't realize that my husband was with another woman, what else am I missing?

The juxtaposition of what you thought was real and the truths you are now uncovering are bound to collide, causing you tremendous anguish. These discoveries inevitably awaken a maddening need to determine what was real and what was a lie. You are trying to figure out the reality of the world you actually occupied... not the world you *thought* you were living in.

But he probably didn't tell you the entire truth when he confessed (or when you caught him). As you quiz him and dig into his electronic records, you discover more and more pieces of the puzzle. This further erodes your sense of security.

To make things worse, your husband might question why you can't get past this. He doesn't understand why every new piece of information that you discover sends you back to square one (emotionally).

The problem is a common one: the affair has changed you. Not only has it changed you, but it has changed the relationship in its entirety. Trust, security, dreams for the future... it's all up in the air now.

Summary: You Will Survive
You probably aren't sure if the relationship can recover. That in itself is incredibly life-altering. However, whether the relationship survives or ends, you have been changed, and you need to learn how to survive with this new information.

Survival depends on understanding what has happened to you and what you can do in response. That's exactly what this next chapter explores.

Chapter Two:
Hit By A Mac Truck
—The Effects of Trauma

When you look in the mirror, you wonder who you've become. You used to be so confident and self-assured; after all, you were sure your husband would never cheat on you. Other men cheat on other women, but that's because those women are crappy wives and deserve it or because those women married jerks.

You were different. You had confidence in your marriage. You pitied women who were jealous of their husbands' female coworkers or who needed to know where their husbands were at all times.

Now YOU have become one of those women. You're checking his phone and hacking into his computer. You're demanding he give you a detailed itinerary of everywhere he goes. Maybe you've even put a GPS tracker on his car.

When he is home, you drill him with questions. In fact, you find yourself asking him the same questions over and over again, and you don't even know why you feel the insatiable need to do this.

You gather clues like a detective, trying to piece together exactly what happened and when. You don't trust anything he says anymore, so you search his words, his face, even his body language for signals. When you discover an inconsistency, you hone in on it, certain that there is still more to be revealed.

Even though you know the details of the affair will hurt you, you want to know everything. You want to know what sexual activities they did—when, how often, where. You are desperate to understand why he betrayed you, and the questions won't stop. Everything you see makes you think of the affair, and you feel like you can't trust yourself or your husband ever again.

Have you gone crazy? No. You're just dealing with the fallout from the affair.

Why Is This So Incredibly Life-Altering?

You are currently in a very difficult phase of affair recovery, a phase I refer to as the *nuclear bomb phase.* Why? Because an emotional nuclear bomb has just gone off in your life.

Right now you feel like the world that you knew has been annihilated. You feel like you are freefalling, unable to anticipate what to expect next. You look at your husband and you see a stranger, not the man who has shared your bed. The person you trusted shared his life with someone else, and you didn't know it.

Emotions, questions, doubts, pain—it's all flying past you as you grapple for something solid to hold onto. Something that won't hurt you. Something that feels like safe, solid ground.

You might find this hard to fully grasp, but you have experienced a significant degree of trauma. Discovery of an affair does this to a person; it pulls the rug right out from under your feet. You feel especially shaken because the person you normally turn to when you are devastated (your husband) is the person who did this to you. You have been stabbed in the back, and the person who usually helps you handle pain is the one twisting the knife.

You are likely feeling:

- Helplessness
- Humiliation
- Self-doubt
- Loss
- Depression
- Denial
- Anger
- Pain
- Guilt
- Fear
- Grief

Especially grief. Why? Because the marriage you thought you had is over. What you've got left—if the marriage even survives—will never be the same again, and you know it.

Relief!

In some cases, you may actually feel a sense of *relief*. You might have suspected that he was having an affair for months if not years. Or you may have felt like you couldn't "reach him" anymore. You might finally feel like you have a piece of the puzzle you needed to understand his distance or some of his other behaviors. Maybe you even told him that you thought he was having an affair and he did more than just deny it—he called you "crazy." If your husband did this, you are probably very, very angry. He made you doubt your reality when you were right.

That sense of relief can cause even more confusion. You're furious that he cheated, and you're hurting like hell because he betrayed you, and yet you're relieved to find out that you weren't crazy after all. You were right... but you are so saddened because you hoped you were wrong.

Like You've Been Hit By a Mac Truck

Take a moment and think about your commute to work. Picture that one day, on your way to work, a Mac truck crosses the median and crashes into you head on. Your car spins and flips over and over. You don't know what's up or what's down. Eventually things settle. They take you to the hospital, and you know that you are "safe" from the car accident.

Your broken bones heal. The insurance company replaces your car. But now you have to go back to work, on that same freeway. You'd be cautious, right? You used to trust that the other drivers on the road would follow the rules. Of course you had driven by more accident scenes then you can count. Accidents happen... to OTHER people. Not *you*, because *you* are a safe driver.

But things have changed. Whenever you hear brakes screech or other cars come a little too close to yours, you will instinctively panic, worried that you will be hit again. Right? Why? Because you now know that someone can upset your world in a second.

Over time, your fear will subside, assuming you don't have a second car accident. You'll be less shaky at the wheel.

This is how discovery of an affair affects you. You're not even sure you want to drive anymore because you're not sure your husband will stay in his lane, and the last time he broke the rules, it was a devastating accident. Viewing the affair and the trauma it has caused you as a bad car accident is an effective way for you to understand your own feelings. It will help you view yourself with the compassion you need in order to take proper care for yourself at this difficult time. (Rider, 2011).

You have been hit by a Mac truck and you are experiencing the emotional and psychological reactions that accompany a significant trauma.

Posttraumatic Affair Syndrome (PTAS)

"Posttraumatic Affair Syndrome" (PTAS) is a term used to describe the emotional experience a woman has after discovering her husband has been involved in an affair. This comes from the clinical diagnosis Post-Traumatic Stress Disorder (PTSD), which describes the emotions and behaviors often experienced after a traumatic event.

The symptoms a woman experiences after discovering her husband's affair are similar to the symptoms people experience after being in a car accident, going to war or experiencing another type of significant trauma. They experience a form of Post-Traumatic Stress Disorder (PTSD). (Steffens & Rennie, 2006)

This is what you are going through right now. It's important to recognize this and care for yourself appropriately.

Signs & Symptoms of PTSD—Look Familiar?

According to the Mayo Clinic, the following are typical symptoms of PTSD:

- Intrusive memories that make it difficult to function
- Flashbacks where the person actually feels like he or she is experiencing the trauma again
- Vivid dreams about the traumatic event
- Physical reactions (panic attacks, crying, shaking) as if the trauma or threat is still present

People who experience PTSD are shocked by how vivid the episodes are. They feel like they are back in the scene of the traumatic event, helpless to escape. Their bodies respond with an outpouring of adrenaline and a fight-or-flight response. Some people describe an episode as feeling like they are being held under water and must fight to reach the surface to get a breath of air.

Behaviors that Accompany PTSD
People who have PTSD often take the following actions to try to deal with the helplessness they feel:

- Avoiding anything that reminds them of the trauma
- Coping strategies such as oversleeping, overeating, drinking, substance use or abuse
- Excessive talking about the trauma as an attempt to overcome it

As a therapist, I often hear women lament that they cannot stop thinking about their husband's infidelity. They are frustrated with themselves. The thoughts upset them terribly, and they feel like they cannot control the recurring trauma. Clinically this is termed "intrusive thoughts." Dealing with intrusive thoughts is exhausting and can spill over into all areas of your daily life.

These flashbacks and emotional responses often result in the following:

- Obsessive thoughts about the affair
- The urge to check in on your husband constantly
- Physically feeling panicked
- Falling apart crying or screaming
- Painful flashbacks to the trauma of uncovering the affair

- Feeling like you can't deal with this any longer, that the pain is too much
- Strong urges to destroy the affair partner's life

In order to move through this, you need to understand the "why" behind the specific thoughts and feelings you have been experiencing. Only then will you be equipped to move forward.

Suddenly the Affair is Everywhere

Just like you wouldn't be able to help yourself from panicking after a car accident, you can't help but be triggered by affair reminders. In the beginning, this will seem like every song on the radio. You will notice that TV shows and movies all have cheaters in them. (Where *strong* women *leave* their cheating husbands and *weak* women *stay* in their marriages.) If you caught him texting his lover, then you can bet that you will feel a trigger every time he texts someone. You might not even make the connection between what he is doing and why you are suddenly so angry, but this will happen to you. Over and over and over.

This might make you feel upset with yourself. I know it's difficult, but try not to be too hard on yourself. Think back to the analogy of the car accident. Imagine you just heard screeching brakes. Wouldn't you automatically tense up and prepare to be hit again? The response is automatic. You don't want to stay in that place of trauma but you wouldn't be able to help it. That's what's happening to you, but your reactions are caused by things that remind you of his affair.

Your experience will be more pronounced if your husband tells you things like:

- "That was in the past. Get over it!"

- "Are you going to put me in the doghouse forever?"
- "Will you ever get over this?"

He may try to shame you or get you to shut up by responding in a way that is unfair and unkind. He might do this because he feels guilty and bad about himself. He just wants this to go away. He knows in his heart and mind that the affair is over and that he will never do that type of thing again. He wants you to forgive him and move on like nothing happened. Or, of course, he may be a self-absorbed, entitled jerk who really thinks you should be over it.

Unfortunately, it's not that easy.

I know there is NO ONE who wants to put his infidelity behind them and move forward more than you do. However, the more you fight it, the more you will get stuck. You have been traumatized, and you need to work through the trauma before you can move on. You have been betrayed, and you aren't sure if you can trust him yet.

It may be helpful to explain the car accident analogy to your husband. Then, the next time he says something like, "Why can't we move on?" you can remind him of the car accident analogy. Ask him to consider how he'd feel if the person who just said that to him was the guy who hit him and sent his car rolling. Ask him to think about how angry he would be.

Even if he doesn't get it (he may refuse to or be unable to empathize to that degree due to his ego or defenses), *you* will understand why you are responding the way you are. This knowledge will enable you to treat yourself with kindness instead of beating yourself up over a natural and understandable response.

Summary: Accept Your Response Without Judgment

When you experience these triggers, don't be angry that you aren't over the affair yet. Remind yourself that you didn't choose any of this. You didn't want your husband to be unfaithful, and you also didn't choose your reaction to his betrayal. This is simply the reality of the situation. He hurt you, and you are responding to that pain in a normal way.

Chapter Three:
Intrusive Thoughts
—The Thoughts That Plague You

I've seen a lot of women in my office who have gone through your exact experience. The following are common thoughts and emotions wives have after discovering their husbands have betrayed them. My hope in sharing this is that you will realize that you are not alone; you are not unusual for feeling or thinking the things you do. Additionally, I will give you clinical insight into why you have these thoughts.

"I Hate Him and Love Him at the Same Time. How Is this Possible?"
You will feel a zillion emotions as you process this. You will probably feel most of the following:

- You hate him and wish he'd die (rage, desire for revenge).
- You love him and desperately want to save your marriage (awareness that you love him and want this to work).
- You can't believe the person you love most has betrayed you like this (intense hurt).
- You want to shut him off completely and delete him from your life (desire to numb out and ignore the pain).
- You wonder if you weren't a good enough partner and if this is your fault (guilt).
- You want to point out how unfair it is that he cheated, especially since you also had issues you weren't happy about but you didn't go outside the marriage (defensive and self righteous).

- You worry that if you trust him, he will cheat again and hurt you even more (fear and despair).
- You feel like you are losing your life (deep loss).
- You are unsure if you even know who this man is or if you should have trusted him (distrust).

All of these feelings are normal, and they will come and go as you process the experience.

"I Need to Leave Him Right Now. Only Weak Women Stay."
You may feel like a doormat for staying. After all, popular TV, movies and songs all tell you that only a foolish, weak woman with low self-esteem would stay with a man who has cheated on her. Your friends and family may also be telling you (if you have opened up to them—more on why that is usually not a good idea in the next chapter) that you are a fool if you stay with him.

Infidelity is indeed devastating. It's very hard on a marriage. It requires a lot of work and time to recover. However, it does not necessarily mean your marriage is over.

The decision to divorce should be based not just on the affair but on the overall quality of the marriage. (Atkins et al., 2005) The late Peggy Vaughan stated in *The Washington Post* "Following an affair, more couples actually stay together than get a divorce."

You probably are not in a position (yet) to determine whether the marriage is worth saving or not. You may be under the impression that strong women throw all his stuff out on the lawn, kick him out of the house or go to the affair partner's house and confront the other woman. The truth is, those actions are not an indication of strength, and can even cause irreparable damage. Plus, acting out usually feels good in the moment but does not produce lasting results. Later, when you feel better emotionally, you may feel like you lost your dignity.

The truth is, a strong woman will do the following:
- Take the time to work through her reactions to the infidelity,
- Gather all the facts,
- Evaluate the relationship as a whole,
- Decide if she is willing to see whether the rift in the relationship can or cannot be repaired,
- And THEN make the decision whether to leave or stay.

You are *not* a weak woman if you don't leave him right away. You are a strong woman who is fighting societal pressure and making the decision to use logic instead of being reactionary.

He may not have thought his cheating would affect the kids, but you should. This isn't to say I think you should stay because of the kids. What I am strongly suggesting is that you need to think this through and have a plan. Look at the mess he created when he let his feelings and emotions take over. If you decide to leave him, you don't have to do it right this second. Yes, you are hurt. Yes, leaving him this moment would feel good. However, there are smart ways to leave (consult with a therapist and a lawyer for starters) and not-so-smart ways to leave. Be smart.

Besides, if you decide this relationship isn't worth it, or if you decide you really can't forgive him, you can leave later. There is no reason to make this decision right now. You may make a decision you regret if you try to make one while you are in emotional turmoil.

Slow down. Think things through before acting. You'll be most likely to make better decisions if you take your time.

"It's My Fault Somehow."
You are most likely confronting the infidelity "whys," mentally exploring the vulnerabilities of your relationship. You are constantly analyzing your memories, replaying instances that should have been clues and wondering why you did not see that the marriage was in danger.

While doing this, you have probably accounted for the external stresses on your marriage (work, kids, family, friends, travel, finances, etc.), but you may be more troubled by thoughts of ways you feel you might have failed as a wife. Deep down, you are likely terrified that you are not good enough for him and that his infidelity is proof that he will never be happy with you.

You're probably thinking about every argument you've ever had. Weight gain, division of labor, child rearing issues, work conflicts, lifestyle differences, how much sex you were or were not having... and you are worried that maybe you will never be what he truly wants.

I want to assure you of something: no matter what ways you may think you have let him down, there is no valid excuse for his infidelity. If he was unhappy, he should have told you. If you didn't respond to his complaints, he should have broken it off with you, or, at bare minimum, asked permission to open up the marriage to multiple partners. In other words, there should have been open and honest communication, and you should have had a choice in what happened.

But he took those options away from you when he decided to cheat instead of talk to you about whatever he felt. This is not your fault, even if you have identified ways that you feel you are at fault for the vulnerabilities in the marriage.

You need reassurance from him right now. You need to hear him say that you are everything he wants and more. You need him to tell you, in plain words, that he made a foolish choice which he wholeheartedly regrets.

However, you might not get that yet, especially not if he is torn between his affair partner and the marriage. Right now, while you work through the immediate aftermath of the revelation of the affair, you need to assure yourself that there is no valid reason for him to cheat on you.

Why do you keep blaming yourself? First of all, as you keep asking your husband why, he keeps giving you his reasons, and the reasons he gives likely feed your insecurities. Unless he says, "It was totally my fault. In my self-absorption, I convinced myself that violating my vow to you was okay," he is feeding you the same lines he told himself. He is telling you how he justified what he did. You may start to believe his reasons for cheating are actual reasons rather than excuses (and that's what they are—excuses) for breaking his vows to you.

It is normal to think that the sun rises in the East and sets in the West. You have probably always assumed that your husband is a good man who would never cheat. You may now think that you must have done something to push him over the edge. Most people also believe that bad people have bad things happen to them. Therefore, you may think that if your husband cheated on you, you must be in some way responsible.

It is humiliating to be cheated on. This humiliation naturally leads to shame, and shame leads to guilt. Because of that thought process, you now think you have some reason to feel guilty.

Also, if you allow yourself to feel guilty, bad and responsible for his cheating, it gives you hope for the future. Huh? What am I talking about? It's an issue of control. If you "caused" his affair, then it was in your control. If it is in your control and you can "fix" what you were doing wrong, then he won't cheat on you again.

Why is the idea that this might have been your fault or might have been something you could control so appealing? Because you want to be sure that if you take him back he won't cheat on you again. You want to be able to control what happens because you don't want to go through this pain ever again. And you worry that taking him back after knowing he is a cheater will lead you to hate yourself if he cheats again. You will think, "Fool me once, shame on you. Fool me twice, shame on me."

Unfortunately, it wasn't in your control. Blaming yourself gives you that much-needed illusion of control over the situation, but this is not a helpful way to view things.

"I Didn't Have Sex Enough," or "I'm Too Boring in Bed."
Did he ask for sex, but you frequently turned him down? If so, you may be struggling with thoughts like the following:
- "It's my fault."
- "We hardly ever had sex."
- "I was boring in bed."
- "He told me he wanted more, but I didn't listen."

Women who have low libido often wonder if it's their fault that their husband cheated.

It's not your fault he cheated, even if he wished your sex life had been better. He made a poor choice and went outside of the marriage instead of making it clear to you that this part of your relationship needed to change.

Having said that, understand that sex in a marriage isn't just about an orgasm. It is the way a husband feels connected to his wife and appreciated for the things he does on behalf of the family.

Men are often honestly SURPRISED that their wife is upset that he had sex outside of marriage. They will report that they thought their wife knew and just looked the other way because she acted like sex was a chore or duty. Some report that they didn't even feel like their wife liked them (because of the constant sexual rejection).

My male clients will say that this was their way of being a "good man" and a good father. He tried to get his needs met in the relationship and did tell you. You didn't make physical intimacy with him a priority, so he found a way to keep his family but still express his sexual self.

If this sounds like something that happened in your marriage, the good news is that your husband does love you but misread your rejection as evidence that you didn't love him anymore. The fact that you are so upset honestly startles him. He isn't lying when he says things like he thought you knew or he didn't think you would care.

If you decide the marriage is worth keeping, you can work together to make the sexual and romantic part of your marriage more satisfying for both of you. Please see the Resources section for books on this topic.

This is the most common reason that strong women agree to stay in the marriage after an affair. She recognizes how unhappy her husband was and that she could have behaved differently.

If you knew your husband wanted more intimacy and you did not provide it for him, you may find that this is the starting place of forgiveness. You can rebuild your intimacy together and come out even stronger as you meet each other's needs through honest communication about what you each need from the other.

"It's Not Fair!"

Even though you may not have been perfectly happy in the relationship, you didn't cheat. Now you're in a position where you have to decide whether to divorce him or not.

You have every right to feel this way. It *isn't* fair. You are between a rock and a hard place, forced to make a decision you never thought you'd have to make.

Let him know this isn't fair and that you need some space and time to work through your anger. I like to frame things as you aren't deciding whether you want to divorce your husband because he already broke the marriage. He already split up the marriage when he chose to cheat. You are deciding whether you want to try to rebuild what he damaged.

"It's Hopeless, So Why Even Try?"

You may be thinking, "Why try to save our marriage? He obviously cheated because he doesn't want to be with me."

Actually, men cheat for a wide variety of reasons, many of which have nothing to do with their overall happiness in the relationship. For example, some men cheat:

- To feel better about himself, because he feels ugly or inadequate
- For the thrill of it
- To feel young, because he feels like he is getting old and unappealing
- Just because the opportunity presented itself
- Because he is a narcissistic, self-centered, entitled, philandering jerk

These aren't good reasons. They don't justify why your husband made this horrible, painful, stupid choice.

I'm just telling you that you need to let go of the idea that he cheated because he doesn't want to be with you. Some men *do* cheat as a way to exit the marriage, but *you shouldn't assume that.*

Unless he says he is in love with his affair partner and is leaving you, you should assume he just made a series of stupid, selfish choices that aren't necessarily part of some master plan to leave you.

Dr. Jan Halper, author of *Quiet Desperation: The Truth About Successful Men,* interviewed 4,126 business executives, 80 percent of which had cheated at least once. Only three percent of the men who divorced ended up with their mistress. (And you know what they say: "When a man marries his mistress, he creates a job vacancy.")

You might especially feel hopeless if you had discussed infidelity as a deal breaker. If you had once told him that, "If you ever cheat, I will leave you," you may think that he cheated as a way to exit the marriage.

If he says he wants to make it work, you are probably (understandably) struggling to believe him. You are afraid that he will try for a while—out of guilt or just to look good— and then he will end the relationship, hurting you even more. You need assurance from him that he did not cheat as a way to end the marriage and that he truly lost sight of the consequences of his actions.

Along those same lines, you are also probably thinking:

- If he was so unhappy in the marriage that he did this, why would he ever want it back?
- We promised each other that if we were ever attracted to someone else, we would be honest with one another, but he didn't tell me! (Yes, many couples have that agreement. I don't know one that has kept that promise.)

Many of the men I counsel did not recognize the slippery slope until they were in too deep. What started as enjoying attention turned into something that was inappropriate, and they did not stop things before they went too far. They made the stupid and selfish decision to cheat instead of getting out of the situation and/or coming clean. He really didn't get how devastated you would be.

Time For Another Analogy: Drinking and Driving
In my home state of California, the consequences for driving under the influence of alcohol (DUI) are severe. The first time you are caught, you lose your license. Additionally, there is a three-month mandatory attendance of an alcohol treatment program and regular AA meetings. You may also be required

to install an interlock breath device that prevents your car from starting if you have been drinking. (Have fun explaining that to every single person that rides in or looks inside your car!)

Why are these measures taken? To drive home the vital point that you could seriously hurt, maim or kill someone (or yourself) if you drink and drive again.

This stuff is common knowledge. In general, we all know what the consequences of drinking and driving are. An adult man who has two drinks within an hour and gets on the road will most likely have a blood alcohol count (BAC) above the legal limit.

But let's be honest. As you decide whether or not to have that second glass of wine at dinner, are you thinking, "I might kill someone and go to jail tonight"? No, you don't think about the possible consequences, or if you do, those thoughts flit through your mind only briefly. You get caught up in the fun; you are relaxed and enjoying yourself. You don't think through it very well.

Until, of course, you see those blue and red lights flash in your rear view mirror. THEN it dawns on you how much you have to lose. The unwise decision to take that second drink has changed your life.

That was your husband. Did he know the consequences? Sure. Did he think it all the way through? Clearly, he didn't.

Good men fall down a path of pride. They play with fire. Things begin as "innocent" flirting that is a boost to his self-esteem. With every line that is crossed, a good man fools himself and says, "I'd never cheat on my wife. This is just harmless flirting." A lot of men buy into the idea that "what she doesn't know won't hurt her." They think they are above crossing the line... until they do.

Make it clear to him that he *has* hurt you, tremendously. Let him know he is at risk of losing you. Ask him to show you how much you mean to him with his actions, not just his words. Then watch to see whether he is indeed trying to make it up to you or if he has given up.

"Who Did I Marry? Do I Even Want to Be With This Man?"
The discovery that he has been unfaithful will undoubtedly shake your image of him. Women usually fall in love with men they trust and respect. You are now unsure of who he is and whether he is someone you can trust and respect again.

You may be thinking:

- "He's led a double life. Do I even know who he is?"
- "Did he ever love me, or has it all been a lie?"
- "There are too many lies. How can I trust anything he says anymore?"
- "This was the one thing I *knew* for sure: that my man would never cheat."

This last point—this feeling that you thought you *knew* him, and you now realize you didn't, is unsettling. This new knowledge results in a loss of innocence that you will have to mourn before you can even entertain the thought of trusting and loving him again.

You need time to mourn this loss. It's as if the person you married died, and you need to grieve that passing. Then you can look at him with fresh eyes and decide if you want to continue in the relationship with him, now that you know his vulnerabilities. Only time will tell if you can truly forgive him and love him again.

Give yourself permission to mourn. Take your time. Be gentle with yourself. It's hard to imagine this right now, but in the future you may be able to separate the man from his actions.

"Why Would He Do This to Us? He Has Changed Our Relationship Forever."

You are right that the relationship will never be the same again, but you may find that the two of you will now solve problems you had swept under the rug. Yes, the marriage you knew is over. However, you can grow closer if you work on the marriage together. It will take both of you for this to happen, but it is possible.

"How Could He Do This to the Kids?"

It may be hard to believe, but he may have convinced himself that he had an affair *because* of the kids. Why? Men tell me that they tried to get their physical and emotional intimacy needs met within the marriage but their wife didn't care. Or she would try for a while but then go back to neglecting him sexually.

I have often been told that when men did bring up their needs for closeness, they were met with shaming from their wives. "Don't you see all that I am doing? Stop being selfish." Or worse, she would have sex but say demeaning things like, "Tick-tock, hurry up." Over time this type of contempt becomes demoralizing. Men feel pathetic and hopeless.

So the husband thinks, "Is satisfying my need to feel close to another person worth blowing up my whole family?" They view divorce as selfish.

Their solution is to have an affair. Through an affair, they get their needs met, and, at the same time, their kids still get to grow up in an intact family. And, as I mentioned before, many husbands think that their wives might be relieved that they don't have to have sex with their husbands anymore. They may assume you know about the affair and that you look the other way because this arrangement is acceptable to you. They think you don't want to have sex, and the affair allows you also to have an intact family without placing demands on you sexually. You get a break from the pressure to have the sex you don't want. He is happy, you are happy (so the thought goes).

"I'm So Hurt and Confused! I Thought Things Were Great. We Even Had Sex All the Time. What Happened?"

If you really felt like everything was great, you are probably stunned right now. Chances are you did everything you could, and your partner has issues that caused him to make this poor choice.

This type of affair is especially troubling. You did everything a wife should to "affair proof" her marriage and yet he still stepped out. Men usually go outside the relationship even when happy because:

- He has low self-esteem and he couldn't say no to an opportunity
- He has entitlement issues; he believes that he deserves to get his needs met
- He is a sex addict
- He struggles with true intimacy
- He is an arrogant jerk

You get to decide whether you are willing to take him back, should he choose to work on those issues and change. You may need some time to evaluate the relationship as a whole and decide if you can hang in there with him while he does some soul searching and gets some help. In this case, I strongly recommend your husband engage in professional help. Warning: without professional help, this type of man will most likely cheat again.

"But *WHY*? WHY Did He Do This?"

He likely found ways to rationalize his infidelity (before he got caught and realized how much he hurt you), but his reasons will never justify what he did.

If there were problems in the marriage, he should have worked them out with you or left. If he had psychological or ego issues going on, he could have gotten help from a professional or found healthy ways to feel better.

A lot of men compartmentalize, buying into the idea that "what she doesn't know won't hurt her." By now, he has realized this was not true. He devoted time and energy into another relationship instead of with you. Unfortunately, a common way men justify that it is okay to have an affair is to convince himself that his wife does not meet his needs. He becomes extremely critical of his wife, all the while telling himself he deserves better. After a while he is convinced that he has been deprived and that deprivation justifies cheating.

You may have been subjected to months or even years of him nitpicking you. What you didn't know was that no matter what you did, he couldn't be happy. He was critical so he wouldn't feel guilty about cheating. Now you know what was happening: you were fighting a losing battle.

Instead of focusing on why he did this, focus on whether he is truly willing to do the work necessary to repair the relationship. At this stage of discovering the affair, you won't hear any answers to the "Why did you cheat?" questions that will make you feel better. It will just sound like he is making excuses and blaming you.

Leave the why questions alone for now. You can discuss this later, when you are able to hear them without turning it around and blaming yourself.

"How Will I Ever Trust Him Again? Is That Even Possible?"

He has broken your trust in the most fundamental way. You will need to mourn this betrayal, regardless of whether you stay or leave. This will be painful, and it may take a while.

However, after you mourn, your husband can regain your trust if he learns how to live an absolutely transparent life. He will need to tell you where he is at all times and give you access to all his methods of communication. He will need to share thoughts with you he never shared before and share the details of his day with you.

Summary: The Obsessive Thoughts Won't Last Forever

In my practice, I use something I call the "Kool-Aid® analogy." Remember when you were growing up and your mom made Kool-Aid®? I don't even remember if it tasted like a specific flavor or if it was just called red Kool-Aid®, but you know what I mean.

When your mom opened the packet of Kool-Aid® and put it in the pitcher, it was fiery red. The more water she added, the lighter the red got. If she dumped a bunch of ice in, it would get lighter and lighter in color as the ice melted, right?

The packet of Kool-Aid® is the revelation of the affair. In the beginning, it will be fiery red.

Remember: you have PTAS. Because marital infidelity is a traumatic life experience that leaves a spouse profoundly wounded, your thoughts can become obsessive over the betrayal. Everywhere you go, you see things that remind you of the affair. These things act as PTAS triggers—that fiery red Kool-Aid®.

What is the water and ice? Time and trust. As your husband proves himself to be a trustworthy man, over a period of time, the red Kool-Aid® will be diluted. You will stop seeing reminders. The reminders you do see will become less strong, less fiery red. Weaker in intensity. Easier for you to handle.

If he doesn't prove himself to be trustworthy or you decide to leave the marriage, the analogy still holds true. You won't feel this bad forever.

Right now the Kool-Aid® is fiery red, and you see it everywhere. As time passes, the Kool-Aid® will diminish in color. This won't feel so fiery red. This book is designed to help explain to you what you are going through and get you to a point where you can make a well thought out (and not emotional) decision to have him stay or go.

I know at times the pain will seem unbearable and you will wonder how you will get through it all. Sometimes, thoughts may turn dark and you might find yourself wondering if it would be better to just "not be here anymore". If you do have thoughts of harming yourself, take it *very seriously*. Reach out to a friend and let them know how desperate you are feeling. Call the suicide prevention hotline: **1-800-273-TALK** (8255) where you'll be connected to a skilled, trained counselor at a crisis center in your area, **anytime 24/7.** Their website address is: www.suicidepreventionlifeline.org. You can also go to the nearest psych ER or call 9-1-1.

Chapter Four:
Resist these 7 Urges
(As They May Backfire *Horribly*)

I know you are angry. You are BEYOND angry. You are furious. You are hurt more deeply than you've ever been. You want justice.

All of this is natural and to be expected. However, before you go any further, you need to understand that there are some actions you absolutely should not take, much as you may want to right now. These are impulses that will hurt you or the people you love, should you act on them.

Keep in mind: these are natural urges to have. I'm not judging you for having them. I'm simply helping you rein yourself in so you don't further damage the relationship, your children or yourself. In fact, I hope in reading this chapter you will realize just how normal your feelings are!

Urge #1: I Need to Destroy the Other Woman's Life
I know you hate her.

Of course you do.

However, this isn't about her. This is about your husband breaking your trust.

It really has nothing to do with this particular woman. From my experience, if it hadn't been this woman, it would have been another. When a man cheats, he does it because he is vulnerable to this temptation for whatever particular reason, and the affair partner is not the problem.

The problem is your husband.

Remember the expression "Never let them see you sweat"? If you give this woman your attention and emotional energy, you give her power that she currently does not have. By going after her, you have elevated her to your level.

The affair partner knows that you are "The Wife." Clients of mine who are the affair partner (yes, sometimes I see them, too) will say to me that once the affair is discovered they are sure that "their" man will return to his wife. She will say that even if she wants to be married to him (and that is usually NOT the goal), there is no way she can compete with YOU. *You* have a history. *You* are the mother of his kids. *You* are the one his family knows and loves. Divorcing you would forever change his world. The affair partner is a girlfriend that can be dumped with little consequence.

Once you act threatened, you put her on your level. If you are worried, well... maybe she *does* have a chance.

You may think that she will act ashamed and remorseful if you call her on her crap. She might... but she may tell you off. If this happens, you will be humiliated even more.

If you pour your energy into hating this woman and trying to get revenge on her, you will do several things that are not in your best interest:

- You will give her your energy, and right now, you need to pour your energy into self-care, the kids and determining what you will do next. You will be fine, no matter what happens with that woman. She is irrelevant.

- You will put your family at risk if you do anything like call her up, tell her husband or confront her at work. I know these things sound tempting, but you need to think about what might happen.
- You have now established communication with her. She may now feel free to call you back. Is that really what you want? Ongoing drama with this woman?

You don't know anything about this person except that she shows a complete disregard for you, your family and boundaries. She could be totally psycho. We all remember the movie *Fatal Attraction*. (If you don't, you should rent it.) What if she then brings your children into it?

She might retaliate in ways that you never could have anticipated. You never know what connections a person might have or what insane things she might do to you.

Also, try to resist calling the affair partner dirty names. He will naturally defend her. (Remember, he thinks she is a good person that just got caught up in the moment; she didn't mean to be a home-wrecker.) When you are raging, he will say stupid things like, "She is a good person." This will make you want to smack him. This is the opposite of what you want to see happen.

Also, you want to avoid the "pick me dance" (Schorn, 2012). This is when you try to convince your husband to stay. You compare yourself to the affair partner and find things that make you feel insecure. Don't do this. Stand strong. You need to look at whether or not you want to rebuild this marriage. Remember, if he didn't cheat with her, he would have cheated with someone else.

However, you definitely need to see a picture of her so you know what she looks like in case you bump into her on the street. Aside from that, don't give her your time or energy.

The Double Betrayal
But what if you *do* know her? What if she is (or was) your friend?

This is called a double betrayal. The betrayal by your friend can be as devastating as that by your husband. Many women have told me it was worse. From the bottom of my heart I want to tell you how profoundly sorry I am that two people you thought you could trust violated you this way.

This is much more likely to be a "we were in love" affair. If this is the case, all your power comes from him. You calling her up makes you look worried, which subtracts from your power. In this type of affair, the husband has usually created a narrative wherein you did not meet his needs, which is how he justified falling in love with your friend and betraying you with her.

Your friend bought into the lies and is part of the mess. It's best to cut her out of the tangled web and try to find out whether the marriage is salvageable or not. Send her an email stating that you know about the affair and that your friendship is finished. Make it clear that this is a one-way conversation and that you don't want a response from her.

Urge #2: I Want to Know Every Detail of Every Sexual Act
No, you don't.

You really, really don't.

There are a lot of questions you should be asking your husband, and a lot of details you do need to know, but you don't need to know more than the following about what happened sexually:

- When did the relationship become sexual? (And how long was it sexual?)
- Did he use a condom?
- Could she be pregnant?
- How exactly did he go about deceiving you?
- Did any of your husband's friends know and provide him an alibi?
- Who else knows about the affair?
- When was the last contact he had with her?
- Does she know about you? Has she met you or seen pictures of you?
- Did he consider leaving the marriage to be with her?
- Did he bring her around your kids?
- What did he think he would get out of this affair?

I know you'll want to ask more questions. You'll want to know exactly when things happened so you can relive that evening that you thought he was working late but he was actually at her apartment, but that will not do you any good at all. You probably want to know the details of what sexual acts they committed and if she was better in bed than you. You want to know if he thought she was prettier or sexier than you.

But here's the truth: those details will hurt you. Sex outside of marriage is exciting simply because it's new and different, even if a woman isn't as attractive or young as you are. Sex inside a marriage is special because it is intimate and builds a strong connection between two people who are building a life together. These are two starkly different experiences, and it will not help you to hear the details of what she did and didn't do with him, or how many times or in what locations.

If you do decide to rebuild the marriage, at some point you will have sex with your husband again. Thoughts of him and her will swirl in your head. If you never know the specific details, it will be *easier for you* to move through the stage of "thinking of them." If you know details, it will play like a horror movie in your head. You will think of the specific acts over and over. If you do these same things in bed, you will constantly judge yourself and feel less special to your husband. You will also hear of the things they did that frankly you don't want to do. You will pressure yourself to do those things because of the incorrect assumption that he cheated so he could do them.

If you are worried that you were not pleasing him sexually, that's a completely different subject which has nothing to do with her. Once you have gotten through the nuclear bomb phase of the affair discovery, if the two of you are working towards repairing the relationship, *then* you can discuss your sex life and what you might be able to do to make it more pleasing for both of you.

You only need to know if she is pregnant, because that presents a problem, or if you need to get tested for STDs. (You should get tested even if he claims they used protection. Ask him to go with you and get tested also.)

Again, focus on your relationship with your husband. Reduce her importance by refusing to obsess about her or whatever it was that they did sexually.

Overall, it's best not to know the sordid details. You only hurt yourself by finding out what they did and did not do.

Urge #3: I am So Angry I Want to Tell Everyone He Cheated

I know you need support right now. I know that you are constantly distracted, obsessively thinking of his affair. I'm sure it's infuriating to watch his mother act like he's the golden boy when you go to their house for Sunday dinner, and I know you are dying to tell your sister so she can hate on him with you.

However, I beg you to please NOT tell anyone right now. Not even your best friend. Give yourself time to calm down and look at the long game before involving anyone else.

Why? Let's take a look at the people you most want to tell.

Your Family

If you tell your family, they will give you advice. They will have strong opinions on what you need to do right now. They may gang up on him and tell you to move out or leave him or do something drastic. Why? Because they want to protect and defend you. Hurting you hurts them. Now your husband just went from being a member of your family to an outsider.

Your family might also have a hard time forgiving him—perhaps a much harder time than you will. You may be able to get through this, as many couples do, and even come out stronger on the other side. Your family will not, and that will make future holidays, birthday parties and everyday events (dance recitals and soccer games) very awkward.

Worse yet, they may surprise you by siding with your husband and pressuring you to not get divorced. Yes, this happens all the time. They will tell you to stay in the marriage for the sake of the kids, because of your religion, because he is a "nice guy," etc. This will feel like crap and will make you feel completely alone.

Better to *inform* them of the decision you *already made* instead of discussing it with them and allowing them to have input on your decision. At minimum, wait until you have calmed down a bit. What you say to your family will last forever, even if *you* get over it.

Are you a Daddy's Girl?

If your husband took the traditional approach and asked for your hand in marriage, your husband also broke his word to your father. Your dad trusted your husband to be the new man in your life: to protect you, to treasure you. You may be able to forgive your husband, but chances are your father never will. The better the relationship between your husband and father, the more the trust will have been breached.

Friends
You also should not tell your friends or neighbors right away. Why? Because they will also have strong opinions and will pressure you to do things that may not be in your best interest, depending on their opinions about infidelity. Also, people have trouble keeping secrets. Your neighbor may promise to take your secret to the grave but then accidentally leak the gossip to someone she thinks doesn't matter and the rumors will fly from there.

Warning: The friend you confide in might end up being the woman with whom your husband has been cheating.

Sadly, most women report that they have turned to a trusted friend or two and have felt judged and become an item of gossip. As shocking as it is to you that your husband cheated, it also will be shocking to others. Some may actually delight in the knowledge that you, your marriage and your family aren't "perfect." It will make the choice to rebuild your marriage even more difficult. Why? Because it is one thing to take your cheating husband back, but it is another to feel like people view you as a woman who would take a cheating husband back.

Good people to tell are a therapist, a minister (or his wife) or maybe a friend who does not have connections to anyone in your family or local friend group, and only if she is someone you can absolutely trust to listen without giving advice. If you don't have a therapist, now is the time to get one. You need confidential support from a licensed counselor who is experienced with affair recovery.

I also suggest you get support from Infidelity Counseling Network, a peer network of women who have gone through this same experience. The site doesn't take a position on whether to stay or go, and it is free and confidential. You can check it out at: http://www.infidelitycounselingnetwork.org.

His Family

If you tell his family, they will most likely blame you. As the adage goes: blood is thicker than water. You will get hurt, and if you try to make the marriage work later, they may resent you for embarrassing him.

They may have heard for months or years that he is unhappy in the marriage. They've probably heard his side of the story. If they find out that he cheated, they may feel like you deserved it. They may say that their family member is such a good guy that if he cheated he must be really unhappy and therefore should divorce you.

At minimum, the marriage that once seemed solid will then be in question (if you let them know about the affair).

But what if you know they love you and will take your side? Let's say this is true. You don't want to lose him, so you tell his family to talk sense into him. He does come back. Won't you wonder whether he came back for you or because his family pressured him to do so? You will be insecure and wonder if he loves you.

Men have described to me that they have walked in their home to find their family congregated. They say it feels like a drug addiction intervention. His mom is in tears. He ends up feeling pressured and ashamed. He isn't glad that people talked sense into him. He will look at you and think you are crazy, desperate and pathetic.

In either case, it's best to leave his family out of the picture.

The Other Victim—The Affair Partner's Husband

If the affair partner is married, you may think, "But her husband deserves to know. He is a victim in this too." Yes, he is a victim, but if you are honest with yourself, you don't want to tell the husband because you care about him. You want to tell him so the affair partner's life is ruined. This is not a good plan and can backfire on you in some serious ways.

The following are reasons why you should not tell the affair partner's husband that his wife cheated with your husband:

- Just like you blame the affair partner, this man will blame YOUR HUSBAND. After learning of the affair, her husband might show up at your house and try to beat the crap out of your husband. What if he has a gun?

(Imagine, for a moment, your children in the middle of that scenario.) This is not a threat to be taken lightly.

- She may try to convince her husband that your husband coerced her or forced himself upon her. She will then have to take steps to cover this lie. If they work together she may go to Human Resources and say that your husband coerced her into a relationship, costing him his job. Even if you don't stay with him, this can cost you in terms of alimony and child support.

- At minimum, the other husband will want to make your husband miserable. Again, this does not play out well if you decide to stay with your husband. Just as the two of you have moved through this, BAM! The affair partner's husband starts driving by your house, sending messages on social media, etc. He will blame your husband for ruining his life and may act accordingly.

Leave her alone, for everyone's sake. In general, vengeance won't do anyone any good and can be very dangerous. Focus on your relationship with your husband instead. She is a distraction. Getting angry at her only detracts from the person you are really angry at—your husband.

Urge #4: The Kids Need to Know What's Going On

This is such a bad idea it gets its own special section. This might feel like a good idea right now, but trust me: it isn't. In fact, you need to do the opposite of what your instincts say.

You need to protect the kids at all costs, and that means you should *not* tell them about the affair.

Please trust me, as a therapist who has counseled many adults whose lives have been negatively affected by a parent's infidelity, when I tell you that you should *not* let your kids know your husband was unfaithful to you. This is important, even if they are adult children.

I know you're angry, and I know you may be tempted to want to get the kids on your side. You may want to explain to them why you are so emotionally volatile, especially if your kids are older and you think they will understand.

But you should not tell your kids because this knowledge will hurt them in three significant ways.

First, it will alter their relationship with their father forever, and children (even adult children) are happiest if they have healthy relationships with their fathers. It is natural for a child to want to defend his/her mother. Unfortunately this then turns into hating their father. You may selfishly want them to dislike their father right now, but it is best for them if you allow them to maintain as positive and healthy a relationship with their father as is possible. If they know about the affair, they may never look at their father the same way again.

Secondly, the knowledge that their father cheated will negatively affect their ability to trust in a romantic relationship. Do you want your child to question love when it comes their turn to experience romance? You do not want to do anything that will inhibit your child's ability to love, trust, commit and enjoy love relationships.

Finally, you need to think of what this will do to your children if they perceive that their father's affair "broke" you. You are their rock. You are the one they turn to. It may mean they take in the message to never get so close to anyone that if they are betrayed, they will implode. It can also lead them to preemptively break up with or cheat on a future partner because they (subconsciously) think that their partner will cheat on them.

Right now you're furious. You might want them to hate their father. You might want them to walk away from their dad forever. At the very least, you don't want them blaming you for the divorce. But you need to think about their psychological well-being and put this above your emotional needs right now.

This means you must:
- NOT talk about the affair when they are home. Little ears hear everything. They understand more than you think they do.
- Control your anger at your spouse when they are home.
- Confide in a therapist, *not your child*, about your hurt and anger.
- Explain in generic terms that "Dad did something that upset me, but we're figuring it out." Use age-appropriate language. Do not let them tease it out of you.

I know that you may not even be able to imagine this right now, but you may choose to get back together with your husband. As I said earlier, you may forgive him but others close to you may not be able to forgive him. This includes your children. You might never be able to put your FAMILY back together. They may always resent their father and they may not recommit to the family.

You are a mother. You know how to put your kids' needs ahead of your own. Really, think long term here.

What if they already know? If they know, there isn't anything you can do about it. It is important for you to emphasize that they do not need to protect you or hate their dad. One of the single most damaging things you can do is make your child feel that when they are with you, they have to hate their father.

Urge #5: Spidey Senses are Going Off and You Look Through All His Stuff

Don't go through his phone when you feel bad about yourself.

Here is the thing: if you feel bad about yourself and you go looking for things, you will find them. Countless women have read to me (or shown me screenshots of) innumerable texts, emails and Facebook messages of things they found on their man's phone. The overwhelming majority of these messages were nothing. Nothing. Nothing. But since the wife already felt bad about herself, she read the tea leaves as showing that her husband was still having an affair. Then, of course, she will go to her husband. He will have a rational explanation... and of course now he knows you are checking his phone. If he is being shady, he will know to delete stuff in the future.

Ladies, I am not saying don't go through his stuff. I only mean don't do it when you are emotional. Here's a better strategy. As you read this book, pick a date on a calendar and tell yourself that is the time you will go through his stuff. Maybe every Thursday you rifle through everything. Why does this strategy work better? Because you do not feel bad about yourself, you are less likely to jump to incorrect conclusions. You will be more rational while looking for evidence.

Now, let's say you do find something. My advice is to sit on the information unless it is clearly a cheating message. Why? Because then you can look at his phone again. Is the message you were worried about now deleted? Suspicious! Is there more to the conversation? If he doesn't know that you are checking on him, he will continue the conversation and then you will really know the situation. Don't blow it by being insecure and impatient.

You may think it's strange that I say, "Don't blow it." Let me explain: the wives I've counseled have often been very clever on how they have kept track of their husbands, which is good—you need to check up on him. He has proven himself to be untrustworthy, and you need to check (from time to time) to assure yourself that he is staying faithful (and to catch him if he is not). However, if you reveal your methods of checking up on him to your husband over stupid nothings, he will know how you are figuring things out. Then, if he is hiding things, he will change his behaviors and you won't know what's really going on. I want you to keep your methods of tracking his repentance (or lack thereof) secret.

Keeping this in mind, don't blow it by going back into his email and uncovering more about the affair (in the past). Yes, he has had an affair. No, he hasn't told you the full extent of it. It would be very rare if he came clean with all the details.

If you dig back through old emails, you will find both big things and small things. The problem is this: if you do this, you will obsess about even little details. It will be hard to resist bringing up these inconsistencies in an effort to uncover more information, but try to resist doing this because it will just hurt you more. None of it will make you feel better.

What you want to do is make sure he isn't still in a relationship with his affair partner or is cheating on you (in the future). Don't reveal how you discover these things or he will alter his ways.

Urge #6: I'm Going to Cheat on Him and See How He Likes It

This is called a "revenge affair." I know this sounds like a tempting idea. You want to hurt him as much as he hurt you, and you can't think of any other way to do so. If you've been flirting with someone, it might also be tempting to use your husband's infidelity as an excuse for acting on your own desires.

In either case, it's not a good idea.

The mess you make will be much harder to clean up than the mess you're already in.

I know; it's not fair. However, if you want to give the marriage a chance, you need to remain faithful to him. Again, vengeance is not helpful. It only causes more pain and damage, and the consequences can be devastating.

There are two important reasons why a revenge affair is not a good idea.

First of all, your husband might leave you.

You don't know how your husband will take the fact you slept with another man. Hypocritical, I know. But men tend to replay the scenario not as your act of revenge but of another man defiling his wife.

He will leave because although he knows his cheating meant nothing, he believes your cheating must clearly mean you don't love him. As a woman, you wouldn't be able to have sex with someone else if you were still in love with him.

If you cheat on him, your actions will "show" him that what he did was so bad there is no hope left for the marriage surviving and he may give up. If anyone decides, it should be YOU, if and when YOU determine that the marriage is not worth saving. Do not give him this power.

Secondly, you lose the high road.

If you cheat, you may feel better and believe that things have been equalized. However, your husband's infidelity will still hurt you. Now, you have no "right" to be upset because you have cheated too. The whole "but you cheated first" argument doesn't hold up.

Most importantly, you lose your dignity. Right now you are not a cheater. Are you really going to let his actions determine your character? Do you think five years from now you will be proud of becoming a cheater?

Instead of retaliating, take a deep breath and start evaluating your marriage from a bird's eye point of view. Keep the focus on the marriage, and keep it simple.

Urge #7: I Need to Punish Him as Much as I Can. I'm Not A Doormat!

When you're hurting this badly, you want to hurt the person who injured you. That means you want to make your husband feel as much pain as possible. Also, you probably fear that if you don't get really angry he will think you are a doormat and believe that he can do this again to you in the future.

I understand. This is a natural response to being hurt.

Sometimes, lashing out at him isn't even conscious. I know it's hard to believe this now, but there will be a time when the two of you have fun again (if you choose to work things out), and you may, after that good time together, suddenly struggle with the desire to punish him.

Let me explain what happens: You have a nice evening. He is holding you in his arms. You feel safe. You feel good.

Then you snap. Suddenly you are furious and want to hurt him. Why?

You do this because you are worried that he will think you have forgiven him and that he "got away" with having an affair.

Try not to do this. Instead of blowing up at him, let yourself have that positive moment. Realize why you go from comfortable to raging at your husband, and try to coast through the urge to punish him. Instead, give yourself permission to enjoy the fact that you are healing.

At other times, you may wish to hurt him because you are still taking out your pain on him. I urge you to consider your long-term goals instead of gratifying your short-term desires to see him squirm.

Why? Because a lot of men who have cheated are afraid to come clean with their wives for this exact reason: they fear that they cannot handle being in the doghouse forever.

Your husband needs to believe that forgiveness and restitution are possible. If he thinks you will hold this over his head forever, he might not have the courage to work through this hard time with you. He might decide this is too difficult and he has screwed up too badly, and he might give up.

Make it clear that you expect complete transparency and commitment to the relationship. Explain to him that you are evaluating the relationship to decide whether you want to try to make this work or not, and put yourself in a position of power. If he does not prove himself to be sorry and absolutely committed, you will leave.

However, you also will want to assure him that there is hope. He needs to know there is light at the end of the tunnel. He needs to believe that if he does prove to be the loving, faithful, committed husband you once believed him to be, that you are willing to put this behind you. If he doesn't believe you can forgive him, he won't be able to invest in the marriage emotionally. Why? Because no one can handle never-ending condemnation. He needs hope that you might be able to restore the relationship, assuming he proves himself worthy.

Summary: Think Long and Hard Before Taking Any of These Actions

I urge you to refrain from any of the actions listed in this chapter. If you show restraint in these areas, you will fare better in the long run, even if you decide to leave the marriage. You will have acted with honor and integrity, and you will be able to make rational decisions that you will not regret further down the road.

Chapter Five:
Actions To Help You Feel Safe

You will not feel safe until the affair is over and you know what happened. You need to know what you are dealing with. You have a right to know the life you were really living, not the life you thought you were living. The following actions will help you regain control so you can make the best decisions possible.

Good Idea #1: Ask That Your Husband End the Affair
This is important because it is the key factor in determining whether your husband is truly sincere about wanting to make the marriage work or not. In my professional opinion, if he isn't willing to cut off contact with the affair partner, you should call a divorce attorney.

Men may say a lot of things, but you need to watch his actions to determine whether he is genuinely ready to commit to you or whether he is still hooked on her.

To determine this, insist that he ends the affair, and follow these pointers to ensure it truly happens.

You will want to:
- Be on the call when he ends it with his affair partner. Understand that he cannot control what she does or says, but expect him to tell her that there will be no more contact.
- Ask for complete access to all of his email accounts, text messages, etc. This isn't going to be forever, but you should have access as long as it takes for you to

feel secure. I'm sure you hate that you are now the wife who checks her husband's emails!

- Talk through what you want him to do if and when his affair partner contacts him. I suggest you tell him not to respond at all or to respond with a short "No more contact. I am rededicated to my marriage." Ask him to notify you of any contact and to show you the text messages, emails or to let you listen to the voicemails, if she leaves any.
- Ask him directly if he can promise to never cheat again. Tell him that if he later decides he is unsatisfied with something in the relationship, you expect him to either work it out with you or to ask for a divorce, not cheat. Make it clear that cheating is not an acceptable option.

If he is not willing to do these things, you should be suspicious of his commitment to saving the marriage. You do not want to start the hard work of forgiving him and repairing the marriage unless you know he is completely committed to the relationship.

Good Idea #2: Get the Answers You Need
You've probably found yourself asking your husband the same questions over and over again, trying to determine why he cheated, what went wrong, why you didn't see this coming and what you can do to prevent it from happening again.

This is a critical process to get through, but it can also be maddening—both for you and for your husband. After all, he is tired of answering your questions, and you feel like a crazy person for constantly asking him the same questions.

To get through this, you need to understand why you feel the need to repeatedly ask him questions about the affair. Then you need to work through your questions in a way that will help you stop feeling the need to keep asking them over and over.

First: the *why* behind your need to ask the questions. You've been betrayed, and chances are he wasn't completely transparent when you first discovered the affair. He probably tried to minimize what happened, and you've been asking questions and getting more details with each round of questioning.

This happens because husbands are afraid to tell the whole truth the first time they are questioned. Sometimes this is just a natural "deer-in-the-headlights" response; they get caught, and they fear losing you, so they give you a bland, vague, minimalistic description of what happened.

Some husbands are afraid to admit how long the affair continued or how deep it got because they are over the affair partner now and they don't want to hurt you. They truly just want to move forward. They are ready to be done with it, and so they want you to be done with it also.

Other husbands are just afraid of your response, so they drip, drip, drip little bits of information, hoping that it will be easier for you to hear the whole story if they feed it to you one little piece at a time.

Other husbands are just plain liars who don't want you to know the truth, and you only find out the details if you keep grilling them and catch them in inconsistencies.

So... *why* are you compelled to keep asking him the same questions over and over again? Because you are trying to find out the truth. You want to know what you're dealing with.

You're trying to determine how serious the affair was. Did he love her? Is your marriage and family in trouble? Or was it really just a stupid one-night stand that didn't mean anything to him?

These are valid questions. However, you may find yourself asking questions that don't matter also, questions that aren't worth exploring and will only damage your relationship.

So... how should you go about asking these questions so that you can stop repeating this ordeal over and over again?

First, write down all the information you believe to be true. Summarize all the questions you've asked thus far into the following:

- The affair started and ended at what point?
- Is the affair a threat to your marriage? Did he plan on leaving you and the kids for her?
- Has he completely cut off contact with her? Has she respected the fact that he says it's over? In other words, is she still in the picture, or is she gone?
- What reasoning did he use to delude himself into thinking having an affair was acceptable? In other words: why did he have the affair? And what made him vulnerable to thinking it was acceptable to cheat?

These are the answers that matter for your future.

Of course, no answer he gives will be a good one. You know that it was not acceptable for him to cheat. But you need to determine how serious the affair was, if it will be possible for him to let go of her and devote himself to you and if he can learn a lesson from this. Is he capable of remaining faithful to you?

If you've already asked him these questions several times, allow yourself one last time to question him. Explain to him that you need to know the answers to these questions, once and for all, so you know where you stand. Point out to him that it's only fair that you know the whole truth so that you can make an informed decision. Then calmly ask the questions necessary to get the answers you need.

Refuse to ask questions like, "Is she prettier than me?" or "Did you think about me when you were with her?" or "Was the sex better with her?" Those sorts of questions won't help either of you move through this. Instead, stick to the questions that matter—the questions that will let you know whether you should have hope that the relationship can heal or not.

Summary: Take Action so You Can Begin the Process of Moving On

If you take these two important actions, you will empower yourself to start moving forward. While there are many other actions you should also take, these two steps will jumpstart your recovery.

Chapter Six:
The Stupid Crap He Says and Why He Says It

Let me guess: your husband has said some things you never imagined you'd ever hear come out of his mouth.

I've heard men say plenty of ridiculous things in in my office, including (referring to their affair partner), "She is a good person," or, a personal favorite, "If things were different, you would probably be friends with her."

WTH? You thought it was just your husband that said such asinine things. Nope. It's more common than you think.

This usually comes down to the simple fact that men and women communicate differently. He says things to you that, if you were a man, might make perfect sense. Also, he says things out of ignorance since he does not understand the depth of your pain and how your entire world has been turned upside down.

The following are dumb things your husband may be saying (and how you should interpret them).

"It was a mistake," or "It was an accident."
When men call me to book an appointment, I say a couple of things to them to hold them over until our first appointment. The first is, "Don't call it an accident or a mistake." The second is, "Don't say anything other than 'I'm sorry' until you see me."

Why do I tell them this? Because every man says it thinking it will help and of course it makes things much, much worse. It wasn't an accident; it was a series of deliberate actions to lie and deceive. When he says it was a mistake or an accident, those words minimize the fact that he LIED to you and broke his vow to you.

What he's trying to say is he didn't "mean" for it to happen. He was just flirting and then it went too far. He may not realize that he should not call it a mistake or an accident, or he may not be ready to take responsibility yet, so he says these stupid things.

"She is a good person. It isn't her fault."

This actually may be true. Your husband lied to you, his wife. Why wouldn't he lie to some other woman as well? Many men pretend that they aren't married or that they are separated and are "working out the details of the divorce." These women believe that while you may be technically married on paper, you the wife are aware that the relationship is over and that you are both moving forward.

In rare cases, this statement is actually your husband taking responsibility for his actions. Because let's face it, it wasn't the other woman's fault if she didn't know he was married. It was his fault.

Either way, this will most likely infuriate you because it will sound like he is defending his affair partner and taking her side.

"My affair partner was just a 'friend.' She doesn't mean anything to me."

I know what your response to that stupid statement is. You think that a true friend, no matter how attracted they are to you, turns you *towards* your marriage. That person doesn't take advantage of you when your marriage is in turmoil.

When your husband says this, he is trying to say that he only had sex with his affair partner. He wasn't in love. He wasn't going to leave you and the kids for this woman. She was just a "friend."

"I don't want to talk about this," or "I have answered that already."
Sometimes the guy is just being a jerk, but usually he says this because he is worn down from answering all your questions. He understands and believes that you have a right to know the answers to the questions, but he feels that you are just going in circles. He is tired of talking about it because answering these questions doesn't move you forward.

"You are too angry. Calm down."
If he says this, you are probably yelling at him. He feels like he can't say anything without you blowing up, so he is asking you to let him get a word in.

"I feel like you are trying to trap me."
Perhaps you are catching him in lies, or maybe you *are* trying to trap him. It's possible that you are taking every word and analyzing it to death until he starts to feel like you are ready to pounce on him.

Consider how you've been communicating with him and evaluate the information you have received thus far to determine how to respond.

"Don't tell anyone about my affair."
He's saying this because he is ashamed. It also can be that he knows that it will be difficult to restore the marriage if everyone knows, and actually, he is right about that.

"Why did you look at my phone?" (Or email, or Facebook)
I would take this as a warning sign.

Of course you snooped on his phone! He cheated on you!

If you find something on his phone and you bring it to his attention and all he comes up with is, "Why were you looking at my phone?" in my opinion, he is still cheating.

He has said this to put you on the defensive so that you feel like you have done something wrong. The delay (as you defend yourself) gives him time to think of a lie or enables him to walk away in a huff.

Of course, if it is months (or years) later and he says this in a caring manner because he is concerned that you are still torturing yourself by obsessively looking through his phone, that is a different story. He might be feeling guilt that you are still in pain. Also, if he has honestly been trying to be transparent and you are still obsessively checking in on him, he might be worried that he will be in the doghouse forever and that you will never be able to move forward.

Summary: Why Do Men Say These Stupid Things?
Your husband says these kinds of things to minimize his guilt.

He wants to believe he and his affair partner were just two good people who "got caught up" in something. Statements like these minimize the fact that he committed adultery. To maintain that perception of himself, he has to view his affair partner as a good person. He can't accept that he engaged in bad behavior with someone else who also had bad behavior (assuming the affair partner knew he was married).

How should you handle these kinds of statements? Address the issue directly. Instead of arguing about whether his affair partner is or is not a "good person" (remember: she doesn't matter anyway—leave her out of it), point out that breaking his marriage vows is a serious breach of trust and he minimizes that by saying these things.

Ignore the stupid stuff. Put the focus where it belongs: the broken trust and the path forward.

Chapter Seven:
The Emotional Affair and Why He Doesn't Get It

If your husband had an emotional affair, he may act like you are ridiculous for getting worked up about it. This is particularly frustrating if you feel that emotional intimacy can be more dangerous than physical intimacy. And the truth of it is that, for women, emotional intimacy is indeed the most important facet of a relationship. However, men are different than women and view relationships differently.

What Your Husband Is Thinking
If you caught your husband in an emotional affair, he is probably very puzzled as to why you are responding the way you are. He's probably thinking, "It was nothing! What's the big deal? With all the aggravation I'm getting over this, I should have slept with her!"

Of course, you and I know that had he slept with his affair partner, he'd be sitting across the table from you in a divorce attorney's office because emotional intimacy plus physical intimacy equals disaster!

He may honestly not realize what a serious breach an emotional affair is. You're upset because you know that if you hadn't found out while things remained in the emotional realm, chances are high that the affair would have continued and eventually become physical or even resulted in him leaving you for her.

Why Do Emotional Affairs Bother Women So Much?

Why does an emotional affair bother you so much? And why doesn't he realize how serious it is? The difference comes down to how we are hard-wired as genders.

Sociologists tell us that men and women bond with each other in different ways. However, we all bond for the same reason: we each act in ways that will best allow us to procreate and carry on our genes. (Brase, Adair & Monk, 2014)

So what does this mean? Men instinctively want their wives to be faithful so that they can be sure that the offspring for whom they provide are biologically theirs.

A woman obviously knows the children are hers. Women want to create an emotional bond and be a good partner to the man they've chosen to be with so their children will have the resources they need to carry on their genes.

This is why men are more upset by sexual infidelity—*"Did you sleep with him?"*

And women are more upset by emotional infidelity—*"Did you love her?"*

What If He Doesn't Get It?

Even if he doesn't "get" this piece of the puzzle, he will need to accept it as your truth. His emotional infidelity is just as painful to you as sexual infidelity would be to him.

I've heard a lot of men say insensitive and hurtful things about this topic in my office. They have said things like:
- "Get over it."
- "I should have slept with her."

- "What's the big deal?"
- "You have male friends; stop talking to them."

How should you respond to this?

Explain to him that if he treats the emotional affair like it's not a big deal, you feel like he doesn't get it, which leaves you feeling uncertain that he won't do this again.

When he acts this way, it makes you feel vulnerable. What if he falls in love with another woman and jeopardizes the relationship further? What if next time he does sleep with her? Or leaves you?

Was It Really Just an Emotional Affair? How Far Did It Go?
Let him know that you need to know (for sure) that it was only an emotional affair, and that you need him to come clean with everything. After all, if he didn't sleep with her, he should be able to show you all the emails and all the secret Facebook messages they sent to each other so you will see that they didn't have a hotel room booked and that there were no discussions about how great the sex was, etc.

Then discuss what really happened. Did they say they loved each other? What did he mean when he said those sorts of things? Was he planning a life with her? Was he tempted to leave you for her? What did he get from the relationship?

I know the question that plagues you is: "If I hadn't found out, would he have gone further?" Of course, you will never know. However, sometimes a man gets caught up in the fantasy, but when it comes down to it he really doesn't have the nerve to do it. The flattery and attention felt good, but he wouldn't have let it cross over into being physical. I don't know your husband. I don't know if he would have gone farther. But I do know that it is possible for someone to engage in an emotional affair and then chicken out.

Getting Help

As with physical affairs, men who have emotional affairs usually have issues to work through that may be completely independent of the relationship with you. In many cases, they are overwhelmed by the demands of work or life in general and use the emotional affair as a fantasy, an ego boost or a reprieve from whatever is getting them down.

Summary: Working Through an Emotional Affair

He may never truly "get" why you are so upset by the emotional affair, but the two of you may be able to work through it if you explain what you need from him. Let him know that the way to winning back your heart is openness and humility. If he can prove to you that the affair was limited, and if he can commit to sharing himself (emotionally) only with you, then you can trust him to move forward together.

Chapter Eight:
10 Practical Steps to Take to Save Your Sanity

Now, let's be clear. Your husband cheated on you. It sucks. It hurts. It is traumatic.

If you were a client in my office, I would write you a prescription for two weeks of hot fudge sundaes and margaritas.

Then, however, I would tell you that it was time to take charge of your life instead of letting his crappy actions bring you down.

Now that you know why you have been feeling crazy, you can take practical steps to get back to feeling like yourself again.

This will take time, but you *can* do this. You *can* and you *will* recover.

To end the emotional roller coaster, take the practical steps listed in this chapter. These are actions that will help you move through the difficult emotions and figure out what you want to do.

1. Get a Housekeeper and a Babysitter

I'm serious. You are in a constant state of pain. Time away from the kids and housework will help you move through this better.

Worried about how much it costs? If your husband is truly repentant, he should be looking for ways to take care of you. And how much did your husband spend on his affair partner? Yeah... don't feel too guilty.

2. Get Tested for STDs
Your husband has shown horrible judgment. I don't care if he said they "just kissed." Get tested now.

In my practice, I often also see the affair partner. Almost universally, affair partners report that they *do not* use a condom. Why? Because he is married. He is safe. Often they have been told that the two of you weren't having sex.

Because of a woman's anatomy, certain STDs aren't obvious. For example, genital warts (HPV) can be hidden, but HPV is linked to cervical cancer. *Cancer.* Don't be in denial; don't be embarrassed. Just get checked NOW.

Let him know you are getting tested and insist that he also gets tested. Pay extra for the herpes test (it is often asymptomatic, meaning it is possible that neither of you experience symptoms). Ask to see his test results.

How will this help you stop the emotional roller coaster?

The test results will help you quantify how much damage has been done to this aspect of the relationship. You will find out once and for all if you have been affected in any lasting way (and can get treated if you have contracted a treatable STD), and you will find out if he has contracted anything that will affect your relationship long term. For example, if you discover that he has herpes and you do not, you may wish to abstain from sexual contact with him until you have decided you are sure you want to make the marriage work.

This will also act as a reality check for your husband. It will help him see the extent of the damage he has done. He put you at risk of an STD. You now have to go through the experience of getting tested, and he also has to put himself through that experience.

If you think he is truly interested in repairing the relationship (and you think you might be willing to accept him back), ask him to come with you and get tested at the same time. Ask him to be the one explaining to the doctor why you need to be tested.

This will act as a test: Is he willing to humble himself and take responsibility for what he has done to you? If so, that is a good sign that there is hope for the relationship. If not, well... at least you now know something important about who your husband is. That information can help you make your final decision about the marriage.

3. Gather All Financial Documents
Don't be so consumed with finding additional proof of the affair. He did it. He lied. None of this is news.

Instead of obsessing about the deception, spend your time gathering information regarding your bank accounts, tax returns, credit cards statements and retirement plans. Print out copies and file them somewhere secret. Document amounts, account numbers and passwords. Look at account histories to see if money disappeared to suspicious places.

Run your credit report. Run his credit report. File copies of both.

You should do this for two reasons: to get a hold of yourself emotionally (by taking back your power) and to protect yourself. If he lied and cheated on you, why wouldn't he spend money on her or hide money in case he left you?

Once you know where the money has been going and what the current financial situation is, you will be in a much better position for the future. If he changes passwords or moves money, you will be able to point to the evidence when determining things like child support and alimony. This knowledge will help you feel more secure, regardless of whether you stay with him or choose to leave.

While you are at it, make sure you have a separate bank account at a bank other than where your joint household account is. At some point you may want to start direct depositing your paycheck in there. It might be a good idea to put some money away now.

4. Schedule Time to Freak Out and Obsess

I've already mentioned that one of the symptoms of Post Traumatic Affair Syndrome is intrusive and obsessive thoughts. What do you do when you feel that the thoughts are consuming all of your time? Schedule time to freak out.

I'm serious. Look at your calendar and schedule time to just sit and obsess about what happened. Write about it in a journal. How many times a day? In the beginning, let yourself obsess once an hour. After a couple of weeks have passed (or however long it takes), if you get through an hour and don't even realize that it is the time to stop and obsess, then challenge yourself to obsess only once every two hours. Then three. You get the idea.

Put a rubber band on your wrist. Every time you begin to go down a dark path, snap the rubber band around your wrist. Not too hard, but enough that it stings. Why? This brings you into the NOW. It is difficult to worry about the future or get depressed about the past when you are focused on the now. When you feel that sting, remind yourself that you already have time scheduled when you are allowed to freak out. Tell yourself, "No, not now. You can obsess in 10 minutes."

5. Invest in Self-Care

As you work through these feelings, you need to invest extra time in actions that help you become stronger and healthier. The following are good guidelines to follow:

- Make sure you get enough sleep.
- Try to go for walks. Get outside and soak in sunshine and fresh air. Aim for 20 minutes a day (assuming the weather cooperates).
- Eat healthfully.
- Ask for help with the kids and household duties.
- Get massages, acupuncture, energy healing or take naps—whatever makes you feel pampered and relaxed.
- Incorporate daily stress relief habits like yoga, meditation, stretching or listening to calming music (or a sound machine set to rain or ocean waves).
- Engage in things you like to do. Do you like to watch movies? Read? Paint? Make time for activities that have brought you joy in the past and can distract you from the struggles of the present.

By taking care of yourself, you increase your ability to make a better decision regarding whether to continue in the marriage. You want to feel *strong* in whatever decision you make, not pathetic or desperate.

6. Start Therapy

I know I mentioned this earlier, but some of you may think one visit with the pastor or one appointment with a therapist is all you need.

You're going to need ongoing help for a while. See a therapist to help you gain clarity regarding what you want to do. No, you aren't crazy. No, this isn't your fault. But you need someone to explain what you are feeling and help you anticipate what to expect.

This isn't over yet. Your husband may change his stance as time passes. He may become defensive and start blaming you, especially if he resents giving up the affair partner or wants to justify his continuing feelings for her. He may become accommodating and work hard to win you back.

Your feelings will also change, sometimes from moment to moment. You will need help interpreting his actions and words. You need someone objective (and experienced) who can help you see through the fog, process your feelings and stay emotionally stable as you deal with the ever-changing landscape of affair recovery.

Start therapy now. You need one person that is not in your "real life" with whom you can be totally honest regarding what his affair has done to you. The angry feelings, the sad feelings and the dark feelings. The sooner you dive in, the sooner you will find serenity and empowerment.

If you contact me at TherapyBurbank@gmail.com I will help you find a therapist near you or we can discuss personal coaching options with me delivered by Skype or Facetime.

7. Start a Confidential Journal

Yes, I am sure you have heard this suggestion before, but it really is a good idea for several reasons.

First of all, you need a way to process the obsessive thoughts that keep running through your head. You can't stop replaying these thoughts because your subconscious tells you, "Keep remembering or you will forget and he will do this to you again."

But these thoughts are exhausting. They will wear you out. You can think of them as a heavy burden you carry and need to put down.

If you write out these thoughts, you are essentially putting down the load. Your mind takes a break because it knows the concerning thoughts are safely recorded somewhere. It allows you to let go of the thoughts because you can always access them when you need to remember what happened.

Think of it as making a list before you go to the grocery store. If you don't write down the list, you find yourself repeating "milk, bread, cheese" over and over again so you won't forget anything. However, if you write it down, you can focus on other things and forget about the specific items you need to purchase. Of course, what you are going through isn't as simple as a grocery list, but the principle still follows.

You will look at this journal a week from now, a month from now and a year from now, and each time you will see how far you have come. It is easy to think that you are back at square one, but when you have written proof what step one was (and step two, and three), you will be able to see your progress.

In addition to documenting the things that have happened (and your feelings and concerns), I want you to write out a list of things you like about yourself. You are more than what your husband thinks of you. Self-esteem and self-respect are about you—you are the SELF.

In everyone there is something I call a "core" self. These are the things you like about yourself that make you unique and special. I am sure being a wife and mother is part of that self, but it isn't the entirety of who you are. Maybe you have forgotten that.

Write down these things you like about yourself. Also, list the things you like to do. Then make a plan to do them.

8. Reconnect with your Friends

Whether you stay in the marriage or not, you will need to have friends. Don't have the time? Somehow your husband made the time to have sex with another woman. He can watch the kids while you go out.

While you are at it, take a look at your friend group. Are they all married? Do you have any friends that you have lost touch with after their divorce? Maybe you should catch up. It will give you an idea of what life could look like for you.

9. Exercise

I know that for some of you, exercise feels like punishment. You are under a lot of stress right now.

However, if you don't start exercising, you will take care of that stress in less-than-helpful ways: emotional eating, drinking too many glasses of wine, overspending, snapping at your kids, etc.

Exercise is one of the best forms of stress relief possible. You may not feel like doing it, but every time you finish, you will feel tangible emotional relief.

Now is the time to sign up for that circuit training program or to join a dance class or yoga studio. If you have never exercised regularly, go on daily walks for at least twenty minutes each day. Running, swimming, kickboxing and other highly physical classes will help you get out your frustrations. Yoga, Pilates, dance and barre classes will help you center yourself and feel calm and in control. If you can, shoot for a combination of hard cardio and calming exercises throughout the week.

Not to mention, exercise will make you look and feel fantastic. That's what you need right now.

10. Fake It Until You Make It

I know your life has been turned upside down. However, you need to grab life by the horns and take on a survivor's attitude.

You will not get anywhere if you sit at home and cry and/or rage all day long.

Yes, your husband made a stupid, hurtful choice, but you are strong. You are capable. You will overcome.

Whether you stay with him or leave him, you also have choices to make. And whatever you choose, you will use that choice to become a stronger, better person. You are in control of what happens next because no matter what he does, you can make something wonderful happen in your life.

Have you heard the saying, "Fake it until you make it"? That's exactly what you want to do right now. Even if you feel like the rug has been pulled out from under you, you need to catch yourself, stand up tall, hold your chin high and start moving forward.

The following is an empowerment exercise that has been proven to be highly effective in helping you feel stronger, more confident and more capable. I don't know if you have had an opportunity to listen to Amy Cuddy's TED Talk on power positions, but if you aren't familiar with it, you'll want to check it out here: https://www.ted.com/talks/amy_cuddy_your_body_language _shapes_who_you_are?language=en

Here is the upshot: by simply taking power positions, you can increase your self-esteem. The inverse is true; if you assume submissive positions, your self-esteem will drop.

The research proves that if you devote as little as two minutes standing in an expansive high power pose, your body will increase its production of the power hormone (testosterone) and lower the stress hormone (cortisol).

What does this mean? If you fake feeling confident, your body will respond by producing testosterone, making you feel and act stronger and more self-assured.

I realize that this might seem a bit hokey or new-agey. It is, however, what Dr. Cuddy suggests. Did you see that she teaches at Harvard Business School? She's a reliable source, and the exercise she recommends actually works. In a matter of minutes. That's what I call impressive.

Here's the exercise:

I want you to stand in a full-length mirror. Look at yourself. You probably look like crap from crying all the time. You judge all of your perceived flaws as you look at yourself in the mirror, and, as a result, you look and act small. You look and feel powerless. Research shows that if you look this way, you *are* this way. Your power hormone has dropped and your stress hormone has spiked. You are helpless.

Now look yourself in the eye and remind yourself that as crappy as you feel right now, it won't last forever. No one can take away your self-respect or dignity. Only you can do that.

Set a timer for two and a half minutes. Return to the full-length mirror and take a power pose. Think Wonder Woman. Remember her? Put a smile on your face. Put your hands on your hips. Stick out your chest. Shoulders back. Abs tight.

Now concentrate on your breathing until the timer goes off. Keep looking in the mirror and continue monitoring your breathing. If any negative thoughts come into your head, refuse to get angry with yourself or shame yourself. Just re-direct yourself to your breathing.

In two and half minutes, you will have raised your testosterone levels and reduced your cortisol levels. As you go about your day, remind yourself to assume power poses whenever feasible. Take up more space in the room. Stand up tall. Refuse to cower.

According to Professor Cuddy, "Our research has broad implications for people who suffer from feelings of powerlessness and low self-esteem due to their hierarchical rank or lack of resources." That was you, but it is not you anymore. You are embracing your empowered self. The you who will get your life back on the rails, regardless of what your husband does or does not do.

11. Look Your Best

This and the exercise suggestion isn't to "win your husband back"; it is to win your self esteem back. We all know as women that when your hair is done, makeup is on and you are wearing something flattering, you just feel better.

Right now you need to feel good. That means you need to take time for self-care, including grooming, so you feel great about yourself each day. Even if you aren't leaving the house, you need to dress and get done up in a way that makes you feel positive about yourself.

Go through your closet and get rid of all the clothes that make you feel frumpy.

It may even be time to treat yourself to a spa day. Get a haircut and pick up some fun makeup or shoes. Shop for a couple new outfits that make you feel strong, capable and beautiful because that's who you *are*.

Summary: Start Moving Forward

When you take practical steps like the ones mentioned in this chapter, you take back your power overall. This will help you put what happened in perspective. Yes, it sucks. Yes, your husband made poor choices. But you are not helpless or completely destroyed. The accident did not kill you. Instead, you are emerging from the flames of the car wreck stronger and wiser.

Embrace your power, take care of yourself and start moving forward. When a bad day (or moment) hits you, just return to this chapter and decide to put one foot in front of the other.

You will get through the rough times and come out on the other side feeling ready to handle whatever comes your way.

Conclusion:
This Isn't Right, But You Will Be Okay

It is my hope that this book has helped you to understand what you're going through from a psychological perspective.

Discovering that your husband has cheated is traumatizing. It is a life-changing event that can leave you reeling.

Now that you understand why you've felt this way, I hope you are able to take steps to regain your emotional stability and your sense of self. I can't predict whether your marriage will survive or not (or even if it should survive), but I can tell you this: you are more than just a wife. You are a woman, and women are strong and resourceful.

It is my hope that you can gather your strength and take steps to empower yourself as you determine your future. With or without him, you can make it through this. You will be okay.

Warmly,
Caroline Madden, MFT

Would you *please* do me a favor?

If you found *Blindsided By His Betrayal* useful please consider posting a short review on Amazon and/or Goodreads. Word of mouth is an author's best friend and much appreciated. It will .only take a minute, and would really help me get the word out about my book.

Would you like personal coaching? Want to tell me what the next version of this book should include? Contact me directly:
TherapyBurbank@gmail.com
or CarolineMadden.com.

Excerpt from: *Fool Me Once: Should I Take Back My Cheating Husband?*

Has your Husband come back to you wanting it to work it out?
How can you be sure he is sincere?
What if you take him back, and then he does this again?

Fool Me Once, Shame on Him,
Fool Me Twice Shame on ME!

Since you were a young woman you told all your friends that if your man ever cheated on you, you would be so out of there. But life isn't black and white anymore, is it? You love your husband. Sure, there might have been issues, but you know that marriage is work.

You've built a life together. You have a home. You have children. You cringe at the idea of being a single mother and hitting the dating scene. You want to stay married. But then you think to yourself, "Only weak women stay with cheaters. Strong women walk!"

I'll tell you what strong women do. They sit back and let the dust settle. Right now, you are one of those snow globes you pick up as a souvenir when you travel. You are all shaken up, and you need to let some of those snowflakes settle to gain clarity as to what the picture is.

You can't even think straight and you keep going through a never ending loop of ambivalence. You will never get unstuck until you **develop criteria** around if your husband is sincere in wanting your marriage to recover after infidelity.

Dr. Caroline Madden, is a Licensed Marriage & Family Therapist who specializes in helping women recover from their husband's infidelity in marriage. In **Fool Me Once**, she shares the criteria she uses to determine if a man is truly remorseful and determined to save his marriage or if he is likely to cheat again.

Here is some of the information she shares:

5 Things That May Look Suspicious (But Probably Aren't)

5 Signs You Should Give Him Another Chance

7 Signs He is Going to Cheat Again (And You Will Be Hurt Again)

Diagnosing Your Situation (What Exactly Are You Dealing With?) Two Self-Administered tests to help you determine the Type of affair he had and if he is a Sex Addict.

Infidelity in marriage is traumatic and you need to take time to assess the situation. **Fool Me Once** will give you the tools you need to evaluate your relationship. It will help you determine whether you should trust your husband or not and decide if your marriage is worth saving.

Works Cited or Used for Inspiration

Atkins, D.C., Eldridge, K.A., Baucom, D.H., & Christensen, A. (2005), Infidelity and behavioral couple therapy: Optimism in the face of betrayal. Journal of Consulting and Clinical Psychology, 15, 144-150.

Brase, G., Adair, L., & Monk, K. (2014). Explaining Sex Differences in Reactions to Relationship Infidelities: Comparisons of the Roles of Sex, Gender, Beliefs, Attachment, and Sociosexual Orientation. *Evolutionary Psychology*.

Buehlman, K., Gottman, J. M., & Katz, L. (1992). How a couple views their past predicts their future-predicting divorce from an oral history interview. *Journal of Family Psychology, 5*(3-4), 295-318.

Carney, Dana R., Amy J.C. Cuddy, and Andy J. Yap. "Power Posing: Brief Nonverbal Displays Affect Neuroendocrine Levels and Risk Tolerance." *Psychological Science* 21, no. 10 (October 2010): 1363–1368.

Halper, J. (1988). *Quiet desperation: The truth about successful men*. New York, NY: Warner Books.

Post-traumatic Stress Disorder. (n.d.). Mayo Clinic: Diseases and symptoms. Retrieved from http://www.mayoclinic.org/diseases-conditions/post-traumatic-stress-disorder/basics/symptoms/con-20022540

Rider, K. V. (2011). Using a metaphor to help couples rebuild trust after an affair. *Journal of Family Psychotherapy*, *22*(4), 344-348. doi: 10.1080/08975353.2011.627804

Schorn, T. (2012). The Humiliating Dance of 'Pick Me'! - ChumpLady.com. Retrieved April 04, 2016, from http://www.chumplady.com/2012/04/the-humiliating-dance-of-pick-me/

Snyder, D. K., Baucom, D. H., & Gordon, K. C. (2007). *Getting past the affair: A program to help you cope, heal, and move on—together or apart.* Guilford Press: New York.

Steffens, B. A., & Rennie, R. L. (2006). The Traumatic Nature of Disclosure for Wives of Sexual Addicts. *Sexual Addiction & Compulsivity, 13*(2-3), 247-267.

Trafford, A. (1999, March 30). Health Talk: Dealing With Infidelity. Retrieved April 4, 2016, from http://www.washingtonpost.com/wp-srv/national/health/zforum/infidelity033099.htm

Vaughan, P. (2003). *The monogamy myth: A personal handbook for recovering from affairs.* Third edition. William Morrow: New York.

Zemon Gass, G., & Nichols, W. C. (1988). Gaslighting: A marital syndrome. *Contemporary Family Therapy, 10*(1), 3-16.

Resources

Suicide Hotline
1-800-273-TALK (8255) anytime 24/7. Its website address is: www.suicidepreventionlifeline.org. You can also go to the nearest psych ER or call 9-1-1. No one is worth killing yourself for. You are stronger than you know. Please get help.

Recommended Reading
How Can I Forgive You?: The Courage to Forgive, the Freedom Not To by Janis A. Spring

Divorce Busting: A Step-by-Step Approach to Making Your Marriage Loving Again by Michele Weiner-Davis

Not Just Friends: Rebuilding Trust and Recovering Your Sanity after Infidelity by Shirley Glass

Mating in Captivity by Ester Perel

How to Talk to Your Kids about Your Divorce: Healthy, Effective Communication Techniques for Your Changing Family by Samantha Rodman, PhD

Other Books by Caroline Madden, PhD

Fool Me Once: Should I Take Back My Cheating Husband?

In *Fool Me Once*, Dr. Madden shares the criteria she uses to determine if a man is truly remorseful and determined to save his marriage or if he is likely to cheat again.

Here is some of the information she shares:

- 5 Things That **Look Suspicious** (But Probably Aren't)
- 5 Signs You Should Consider **Giving Him Another Chance**
- 7 Signs He is Going to **Cheat Again**

After a Good Man Cheats: How to Rebuild Trust & Intimacy with Your Wife

* *Insight* into what your wife is thinking and why this is so hard for her to get over

* Practical advice so you know exactly **what to do** at this important stage

* **Clear explanations** as to why certain words and actions you think will be helpful might be making this *worse*

* **Two self-administered quizzes** to help you determine why you cheated so that you can get a better understanding of what triggered your affair.

Made in the USA
Columbia, SC
02 May 2023

16018357R00050